Horse Racing Colouring Book

Written and Illustrated by

Cindy Pierson Dulay

Copyright © 2016 Cindy Pierson Dulay

All rights reserved.

ISBN: 1535586044
ISBN-13: 978-1535586047

DEDICATION

This book is dedicated to all the horse racing fans out there who have visited my website, www.horse-races.net, and enjoyed my photos over the past 20 years. I hope you enjoy colouring my drawings which were all done using my photos as models.

ABOUT THE AUTHOR/ILLUSTRATOR

Cindy Pierson Dulay, a life-long horse racing fan, has been the owner and operator of the website www.horse-races.net since 1994, providing horse racing news, information, and photos. She was the first person ever to be credentialed at a racetrack for an internet only publication way back in 1998. She has won both an Eclipse Award in the US and a Sovereign Award in Canada for her photographs and attends the Kentucky Derby and Breeders' Cup every year.

Please colour this book however you like. Use coloured pencils, markers, paints, or crayons. The colours and shadings are all up to you. Feel free to add in backgrounds or other details and exercise you creativity to the fullest. There is no right or wrong colour or method!

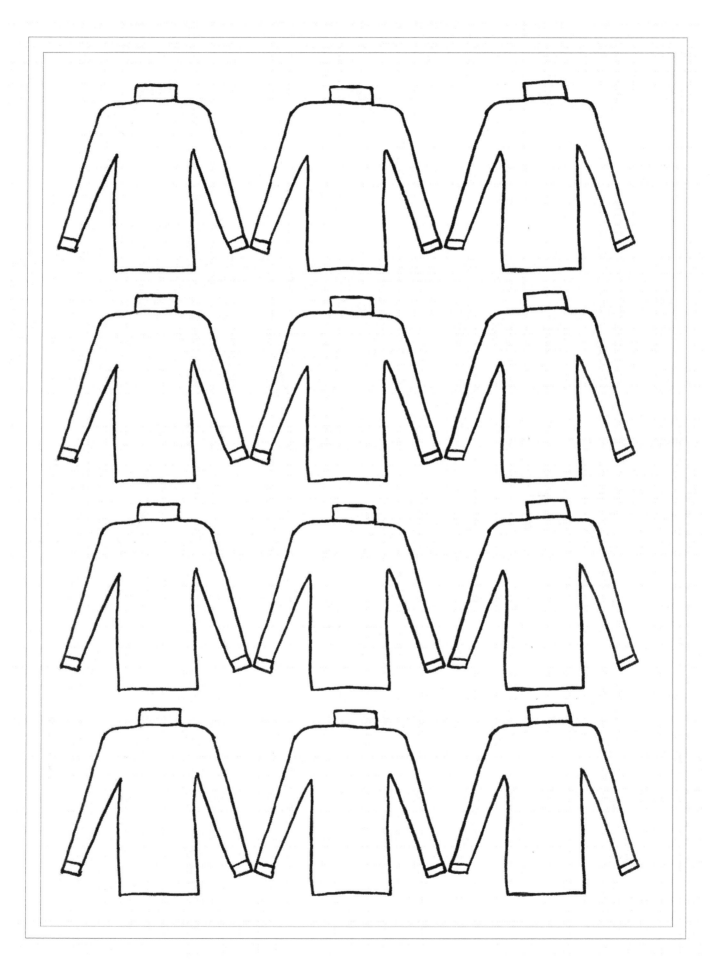

Printed in Great Britain
by Amazon

Awesome Facts about Sharks

This edition printed in 2000
© Aladdin Books Ltd 1998
Produced by
Aladdin Books Ltd
28 Percy Street
London W1P 0LD

ISBN 0-7496-3933-4 (paperback)

Previously published in hardcover
in the series "I Didn't Know That"
ISBN 0-7496-3115-5 (hardback)

First published in Great Britain in 1998 by
Aladdin Books/Watts Books
96 Leonard Street
London EC2A 4XD

Editor: Liz White
Design: David West Children's Books
Designer: Robert Perry
Illustrators: Darren Harvey – Wildlife Art Ltd.,
Jo Moore

Printed in the U.A.E.

All rights reserved
A CIP catalogue record for this book is available from
the British Library

Awesome Facts about Sharks

Claire Llewellyn

Aladdin/Watts
London • Sydney

Contents

Sharks of the past 6-7
Biggest and smallest 8-9
Sharks that glow 10-11
Shark shapes 12-13
Anatomy 14-15
Teeth and jaws 16-17
Feeding frenzy! 18-19
Senses 20-21
Companions and parasites 22-23
Bearing young 24-25
Sharks' enemies 26-27
Studying sharks 28-29
Glossary 30
Index 32

Introduction

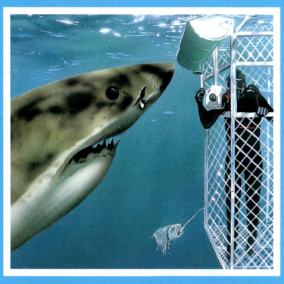

Did *you* know that some sharks are older than dinosaurs? ... that most sharks are smaller than you? ... that some grow inside mermaids' purses?

Discover for yourself amazing facts about sharks – how big the whale shark is and how tiny the dwarf shark is. Find out what they eat, how they have babies, who their enemies are and more.

 Look out for this symbol which means there is a fun project for you to try.

Is it true or is it false? Watch for this symbol and try to answer the question before reading on for the answer.

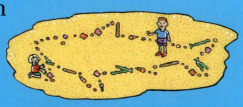

 Don't forget to check the borders for extra amazing facts.

! Megalodon was as long as two buses parked end to end.

Sharks of the past

Sharks are older than the dinosaurs. Their ancestors lived about 200 million years before the dinosaurs. Some early sharks were giants with spines on their head.

SEARCH & FIND Can you find five trilobites?

Few sharks turned into *fossils*, but their teeth did! This tooth (left) measures twelve centimetres and belonged to a monster shark called megalodon. A great white shark's tooth is half this size.

Cladoselache lived about 350 million years ago, and measured about two metres from teeth to tail. The shark's mouth was at the tip of its snout, not tucked underneath as in most sharks today.

Cladoselache

This fossil of a shark called stethocanthus shows that it had thorny spines. Fossils of sharks are rare because their skeletons are made not of bone but *cartilage*, which rots away before it can fossilize.

! Port Jackson sharks still have spines, just like their ancestors did.

! In winter, basking sharks *hibernate* on the seabed.

To see how big a whale shark really is, try making one in the park or on the beach. Using a one-metre stick as a guide, measure out its length and then fill in the outline with pebbles or twigs.

The basking shark is the world's second largest fish. It swims with its mouth open, to catch microscopic sea creatures.

Biggest and smallest

The whale shark measures up to 13 metres and is the largest fish in the sea. This gentle giant feeds peacefully, filtering tiny plants and animals from the water.

SEARCH & FIND & SEARCH & FIND
Can you find three divers?

Whale shark

The dwarf shark is just 15 cm long, not much bigger than a goldfish. In fact, half of all known sharks measure less than one metre.

! Whale sharks are so gentle that divers can ride on them.

Megamouth shark

10

Sharks that glow

Some sharks that live in the deep, dark parts of the ocean make their own light. The jaws of a megamouth shark give out a silvery glow. This probably attracts tasty shrimps.

Can you find six jellyfish? SEARCH & FIND

! The frilled shark has elongated eyes to see in the murky depths.

❗ Cookie-cutters glow green for three hours after they're caught.

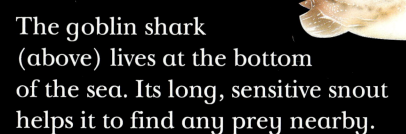

The goblin shark (above) lives at the bottom of the sea. Its long, sensitive snout helps it to find any prey nearby.

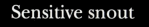
Sensitive snout

Lantern sharks (left) glow in the water thanks to a shiny slime on their skin. Experts think the colouring may help sharks to attract their prey or keep their place in a shoal.

The cookie-cutter shark gets its name from its curious bite. When the shark attacks another animal, it leaves a wound that is perfectly round – just like a cookie.

The wobbegong is a strange-looking shark with speckled skin and tassels that make it look like a rock or seaweed. The fish makes use of this brilliant *camouflage* by hiding on the seabed and snapping up fish.

Stingray

Gill slits

Sharks are related to *rays* (right). Both groups of fish have gill slits instead of flaps, and skeletons of cartilage rather than bone.

True or false?
Some sharks have wings.

Answer: **True**
The angel shark's large fins (left) are just like wings. It uses them to glide along the seabed as it searches for *crustaceans* and fish.

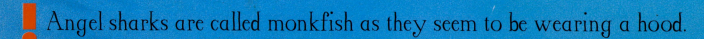

! Angel sharks are called monkfish as they seem to be wearing a hood.

! The wobbegong was named by the Aborigines of Australia.

Shark shapes

Sharks come in all shapes and sizes. The hammerhead shark has a T-shaped head just like the top of a hammer. As the shark swims, it swings its head from side to side so that it has an all round view.

Great hammerhead shark

! The pectoral fins give a shark lift, just like the wings on a plane.

A shark's body is sleek, *streamlined* and built for speed. Its fins are large and rather stiff. They help it to power forwards, stay upright, steer and stop.

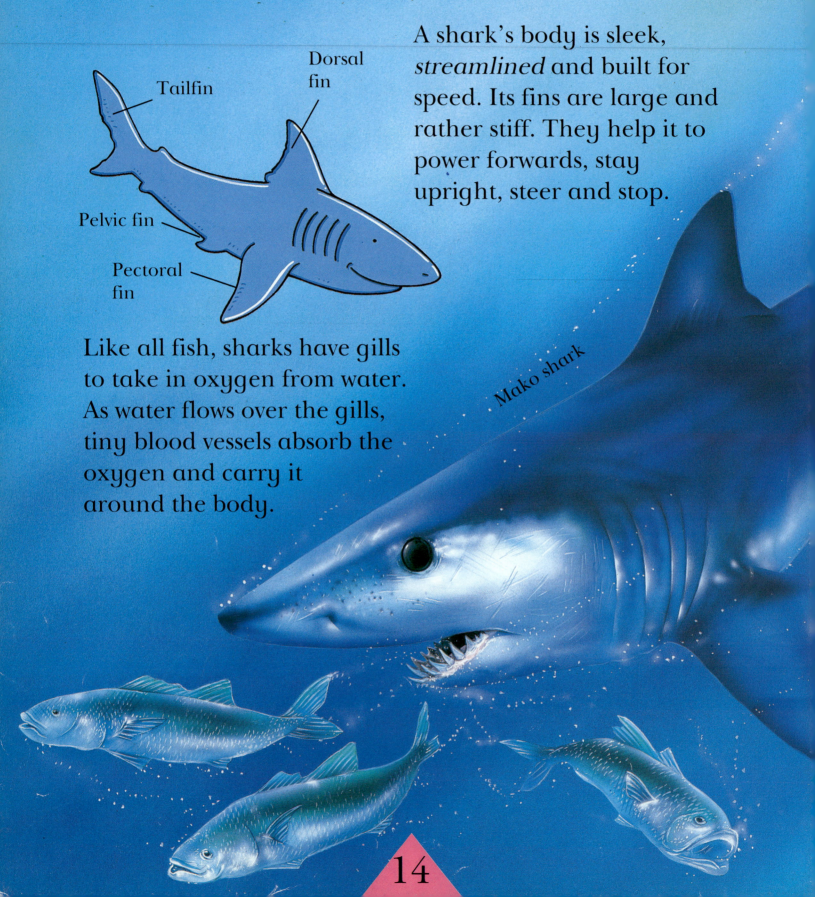

Tailfin
Dorsal fin
Pelvic fin
Pectoral fin

Like all fish, sharks have gills to take in oxygen from water. As water flows over the gills, tiny blood vessels absorb the oxygen and carry it around the body.

Mako shark

Anatomy

Most bony fish have an air-filled bag called a swim bladder, which helps to keep them afloat. Sharks don't have swim bladders, so to avoid sinking, most sharks have to swim all the time, like treading water.

True or false?
Sharks sleep in caves.

Answer: **True**
The white-tip reef shark is a dozy fish. At night, it cruises sluggishly round coral reefs, and spends the day sleeping on the seabed. It often hides away in caves to avoid being spotted and disturbed.

 The triangular dorsal fin is the first sign of an approaching shark.

❗ Fighter planes have been decorated with sharks' teeth to make them look mean.

Teeth and jaws

Sharks often lose their teeth as they attack their prey, so new teeth constantly grow inside their mouth. Slowly the new teeth form and move outwards to replace the old ones.

SEARCH & FIND & SEARCH & FIND — Can you find five teeth?

Sand tiger shark

A tiger shark can open its jaws so wide that its bite is enormous. The teeth have a sharp point and two *serrated* edges – just perfect for seizing and slicing prey.

New teeth form

Older teeth will be replaced

A shark's teeth give clues to its diet. Most sharks have sharp, cutting teeth, but some have small files and filters to trap *plankton* or blunt, broad teeth to crush shells.

Mako

Great white shark

Tiger shark

Whale shark

Nurse shark

Dogfish

Side view of Port Jackson shark's jaws

! Sharks can't chew their food. They have to swallow it in large chunks.

Sharks eat all kinds of foods: seabirds, seals, turtles, crustaceans and plankton. They rarely eat people. They don't like the taste of human flesh!

Blue sharks

Feeding frenzy!

When sharks feed, others may join in. As they snap at the food they get excited by the blood and movement in the water. They can bite or kill each other during this 'feeding frenzy'.

! Found in the stomachs of sharks: a mustard jar, a plastic bag, beer cans, ...

! ... an old tyre, three raincoats, a cigar, an anchor and an oil drum.

A shark's jaws lie a long way under its pointed snout. As the fish lunges to bite, it lifts its nose out of the way, and swings its jaws forwards. Then it rolls up its eyes inside its head to protect them during the attack.

 True or false?
Some sharks attack with their tail.

Answer: **True**
The thresher shark has a long tail, which it lashes in the water like a whip. Scientists think that this either stuns its prey or herds fish into a tightly-knit group, which the thresher shark then attacks.

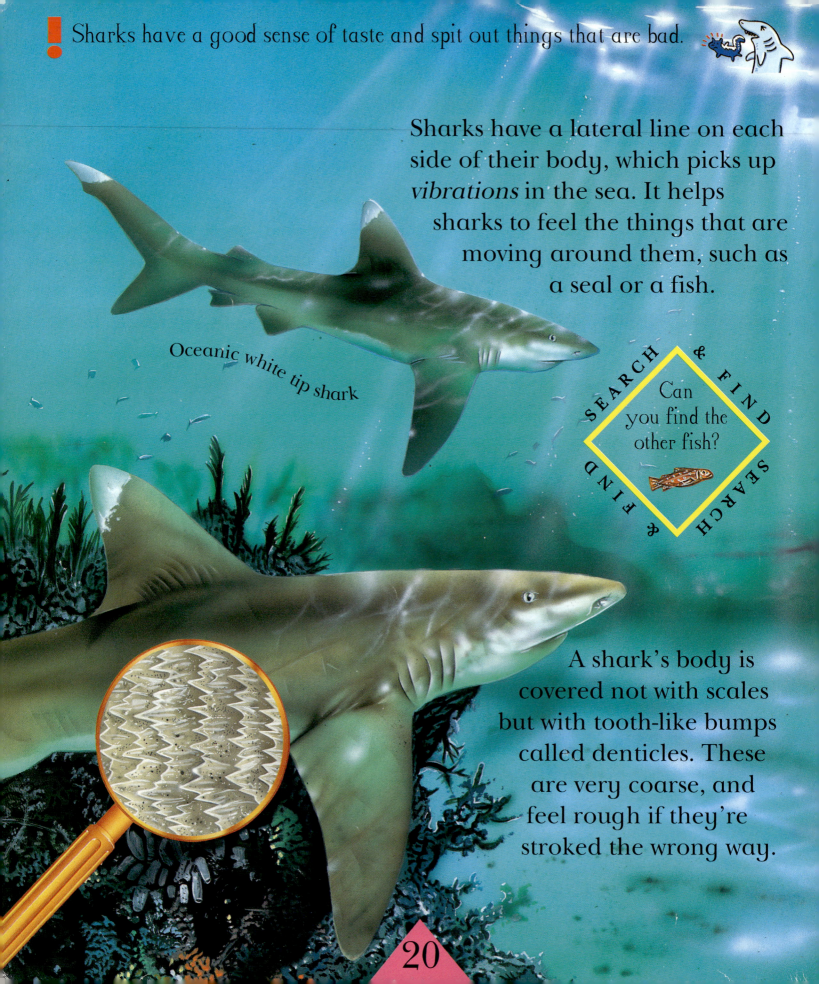

! Sharks have a good sense of taste and spit out things that are bad.

Sharks have a lateral line on each side of their body, which picks up *vibrations* in the sea. It helps sharks to feel the things that are moving around them, such as a seal or a fish.

Oceanic white tip shark

SEARCH & FIND
Can you find the other fish?
FIND & SEARCH

A shark's body is covered not with scales but with tooth-like bumps called denticles. These are very coarse, and feel rough if they're stroked the wrong way.

Senses

Sharks have a keen sense of smell. They can smell blood over a kilometre away. As water streams past their nostrils, they pick up messages in the sea around them. If sharks smell the blood of a wounded animal, they can power towards it.

Sharks have tiny *organs* on their snout that can pick up electrical signals. Since every creature in the sea produces some kind of electricity, these organs help sharks to hunt them down.

! Shark skin was once used on sword handles to give a good grip.

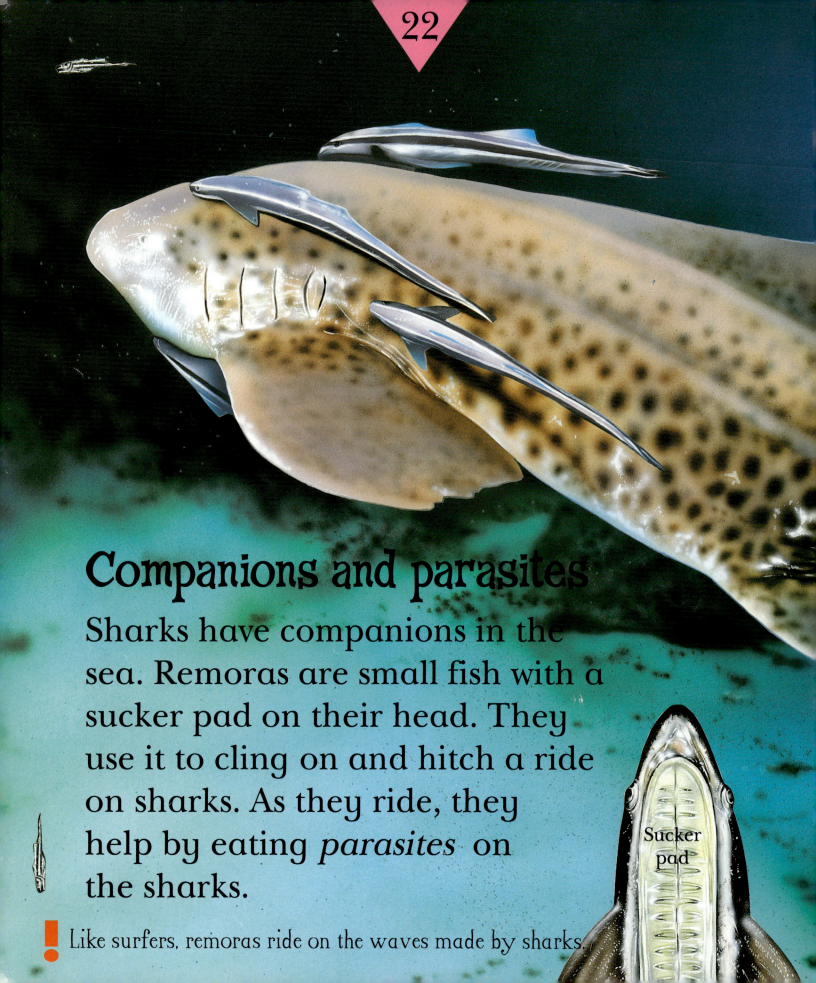

Companions and parasites

Sharks have companions in the sea. Remoras are small fish with a sucker pad on their head. They use it to cling on and hitch a ride on sharks. As they ride, they help by eating *parasites* on the sharks.

Sucker pad

! Like surfers, remoras ride on the waves made by sharks.

! **Long *tapeworms* live inside a shark's stomach and steal its food.**

Small, agile pilot fish often swim alongside a shark. They probably feel safe near their large companion, and can also feed on scraps of its food.

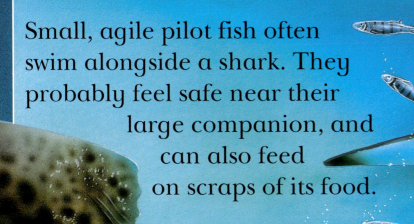

Zebra shark

SEARCH & FIND
Can you find ten remoras?
FIND & SEARCH

Copepods are crustacea that stick to a shark's fins and feed on it. They may even cling to a shark's eye, so that it can hardly see.

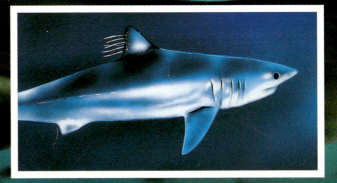

23

> ❗ Sharks' eggs hatch more quickly in warm seawater.

Bearing young

Some sharks hatch from eggs, some develop inside their mother and some grow in leather purses, called mermaid's purses. The mother lays her eggs in a mermaid's purse, the eggs grow into baby sharks and hatch after 10 months.

SEARCH & FIND — Can you find the mother shark?

Swell shark embryos

Three months old

Seven months old

While some kinds of shark hatch out of eggs, most develop inside their mother's body. They feed either on egg *yolk* or on food in their mother's blood, and are later born live, like *mammals*.

A baby lemon shark emerges from its mother.

Next time you're on the beach, try to find a mermaid's purse. The dogfish is a common shark and its dry, black egg cases are often washed up on the shore.

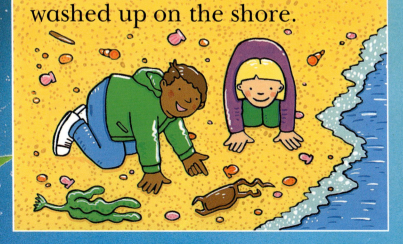

Many sharks try to protect their eggs. The horn shark wedges her spiral-shaped egg case into a crack in a rock. Other egg cases have long tendrils that cling on to plants.

Horn shark egg

! A whale shark's egg is the size of an American football.

Fishermen have been attacked by sharks hauled up in their nets.

Sharks' enemies

People are sharks' worst enemies. Large, meat-eating sharks have no enemies in the sea. But people kill them for sport, and for their meat, skin and oil. Also, many sharks get trapped in our fishing nets, and drown.

Great white shark

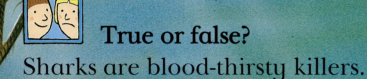 **True or false?**
Sharks are blood-thirsty killers.

Answer: **False**
This is a myth that films, such as *Jaws*, have helped to spread. Most sharks leave people alone. Scientists believe that attacks only happen when a shark mistakes a swimmer for a seal or other kind of prey.

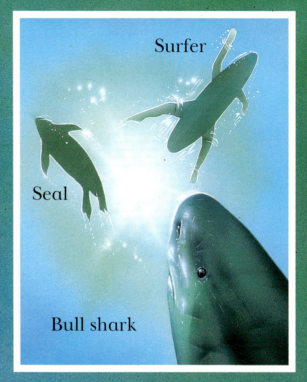

Sharks are killed so that people can make soup from their fins, jewellery from their teeth, and medicines and lipsticks from their oil. Yet all these things can be made using other materials.

Some people catch sharks for sport, and treat their bodies as trophies. Every year, the number of large sharks in the sea falls.

! Sharks seem to attack more men than women.

! You can see sharks in aquaria - but they are better off in the sea.

Studying sharks

Divers who study sharks need protection. Many wear chain-mail suits called neptunics, made from thousands of stainless steel rings. Sharks can't bite through the heavy suits.

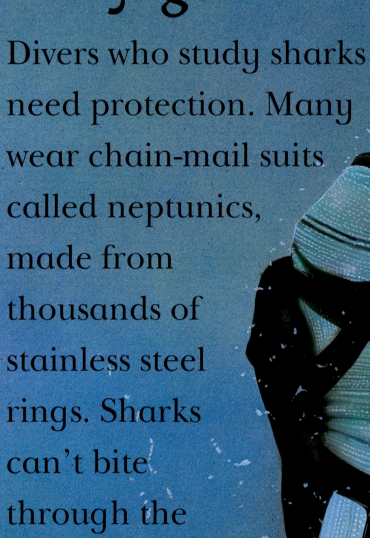

Blue shark

Sonic tag

Tiger shark

Tagging pole

To study sharks, scientists need to be able to follow them. They do this by catching sharks, attaching sonic tags to their fins and then returning them to the water. The tags give out radio signals which the scientists carefully track.

Underwater photographers can film sharks safely from inside strong metal cages. It can still be a scary ordeal, though. They attract the sharks with a strong-smelling *bait*. Sometimes the sharks crash heavily against the cages, trying to get inside!

Great white shark

! The bubbles from a diver's aqualung scare some sharks.

Glossary

Bait
Food, such as a dead fish, which is used to attract sharks.

Camouflage
The colours and markings on an animal that help it to blend in with its surroundings.

Cartilage
The material that forms the skeletons of sharks and rays.

Crustacean
An animal, such as a lobster or a crab, that has a hard outer shell and lots of legs.

Fossil
Animal remains which have turned to stone over millions of years.

Hibernate
To spend the winter in a kind of deep sleep.

Mammal
An animal, such as a cat, that gives birth to its young and feeds it on milk.

Organ
Any part of the body that has a special purpose, such as the eyes which are the organs of sight and the ears which are the organs of hearing.

Parasite
An animal that lives on another animal (known as the host) and gets food from it. A parasite always damages its host.

Plankton
Microscopic plants and animals that live in the sea.

Ray
A kind of large, flat sea fish with wing-like fins and a long tail.

Serrated
Having a sharp, zig-zagging edge like a saw.

Streamlined
Having a smooth body shape that moves easily through the water.

Tapeworm
A long, flat worm that lives inside the stomach and intestines of other animals. It is a parasite.

Vibration
A shaking movement that is often felt rather than seen.

Yolk
The yellow part inside an egg, which provides food for the growing animal.

Index

angel shark 12

basking shark 8
bull shark 27

camouflage 12, 30
cladoselache 7
cookie-cutter shark 11
copepods 23

denticles 20
dinosaurs 6
divers 9, 28, 29
dogfish 17, 25
dorsal fin 14, 15
dwarf shark 9

fossils 6, 7, 30
frilled shark 10

gills 12, 14
goblin shark 11
great white shark 6, 17, 26, 29

hammerhead shark 13
horn shark 25

Jaws 27
jellyfish 10

lantern sharks 11
lateral line 20

mako shark 14, 15
megalodon 6

megamouth shark 10
mermaid purses 24, 25
monkfish 12

neptunics 28
nurse shark 17

oceanic white-tip shark 20

pectoral fin 14, 15
pelvic fin 14
pilot fish 23

plankton 17, 18, 31
Port Jackson shark 7, 17

rays 12, 30, 31
remoras 22, 23

sand tiger shark 16
sonic tags 29
stingray 12
sucker 22
swell shark 24
swim bladder 15

tailfin 14
thresher shark 19
tiger shark 17, 29
trilobites 6

whale shark 8, 9, 17, 25
white-tip reef shark 15
wobbegong 12, 13

zebra shark 23